LOWESTOFT

Produced by The Francis Frith Collection
exclusively for

OTTAKAR'S

www.ottakars.co.uk

First published in the United Kingdom in 2005 by The Francis Frith Collection®

Hardback edition published in 2005 ISBN 1-84567-816-8

British Library Cataloguing in Publication Data

So You Think You Know? Lowestoft
Text adapted from original material supplied by Ian G Robb

The Francis Frith Collection
Frith's Barn, Teffont,
Salisbury, Wiltshire SP3 5QP
Tel: +44 (0) 1722 716 376
Email: info@francisfrith.co.uk
www.francisfrith.co.uk

Printed and bound in England

Front Cover: **LOWESTOFT, PUNCH AND JUDY,
CHILDREN'S CORNER c1955** LI05079t

The colour-tinting is for illustrative purposes only, and is not intended to be historically accurate

CONTENTS

2   Lowestoft Miscellany

30   Lowestoft Quiz Questions

56   Lowestoft Quiz Answers

60   General History Quiz Questions

84   General History Quiz Answers

LOWESTOFT, LOW LIGHT FROM MARINER'S SCORE 1921 71704

LOWESTOFT MISCELLANY

Many earlier writers on Lowestoft believed that Ailmar's church or chapel at Akethorp was a wooden structure. This was despite the fact that Gunton St Peter's in the next parish had been built of flint and stone a century before the Domesday entry.

For most of its documented existence, the town of Lowestoft centred round the High Street. Until the early 1800s, its population averaged around 2,000.

As far as can be ascertained, Lowestoft's involvement in the herring fishing trade lasted from before Domesday right up to the 1960s - well over a 1,000 years.

Until the road widening of the High Street in the late 1890s, there were several buildings that could easily vie for the title of oldest house in Lowestoft. Today, only one contender is left - 36 High Street.

Norfolk and Suffolk are renowned for their round tower churches. However, not all of them are round as such. Gunton St Peter's tower in Lowestoft, for example, is oval in shape and is particularly noticeable when viewed from Gunton Church Lane.

The rediscovery in Lowestoft of the medieval cellars and undercrofts in the High Street in the late 1890s, and the fact that some were quite extensive, led many to believe that a few, in particular those under the Town Hall, led all the way to St Margaret's Church - half a mile away. This was ultimately disproved in 1903, with the building of the railway line between Lowestoft and Yarmouth.

At one time, Lowestoft's Basket Wells, the site of which was between Winnipeg Road and Water Lane, were believed to have been named after Bess and Kate, two old maids reputed to have lived over the porch of St Margaret's Church. In fact, they were named after the wickerwork used to reinforce the sides of the wells.

Although most of the cliff side of the High Street between 48 High Street and Rant Score, Lowestoft, was decimated in the Great Fire of 1645, one building - now 53 and 54 High Street - seems to suggest that at least its facade escaped. The rest of this side of the High Street dates from after the time of the fire.

The behaviour of the town's cannoneer saved Lowestoft from destruction when Cromwell arrived in March 1643 to quell a supposed rebellion. The anonymous cannoneer decided to run after volunteers from Cromwell's army got into the town and fired at him. Cromwell then entered Lowestoft unmolested, and the town was spared the battle and ultimate destruction by Cromwell's forces which would almost certainly have ensued if Lowestoft had put up a fight.

LOWESTOFT, THE ESPLANADE 1887   1983I

In 1676 Samuel Pepys asked his superior, Sir Thomas Allin, to suggest the site for a lighthouse in Lowestoft, hence today's High Light. Although Pepys occasionally dined at Sir Thomas's house in London and liked to travel, unfortunately there is no record of him coming to Sir Thomas's home at Lowestoft.

Until the Lowestoft Clearances of the 1960s, at least one property remained which was directly connected to one of the two women accused in the Lowestoft Witch Trials of 1665. Part of Rose Cullender's house on the corner of Mariner's Street which tended to get damaged by incompetent wagon drivers survived for nearly 300 years after her death.

There is a close connection with the Lowestoft Witch Trials of 1665 and the Salem Witch Trials. Nonconformist families from the Lowestoft area had emigrated to Massachusetts, New England. Nicholas Pacy, Samuel's elder brother, is believed to have lived at Salem for a time.

Lowestoft has had a town chamber of one description or another, since even before the Corn Cross and Town Chamber of 1698. All have been on the same site which is covered today by the present Town Hall.

The curfew bell made from the brass collected by Jessop from St Margaret's Church and the clock mechanism made for the Corn Cross and Town Chamber of 1698 are housed today in Lowestoft Town Hall clock tower. Struck by lightning in early 2005, for a while the clock decided to go backwards.

LOWESTOFT, THE BRIDGE AND THE HARBOUR c1925 L105501

In the early resort at Lowestoft as elsewhere, a 'dipper' was employed to immerse those taking the waters by the old South Beach. Some hardier souls would wade into the sea semi-clad.

At the height of the bathing season, Lowestoft's population would double to around 3,000.

Until the arrival of the turnpike, the only reliable and comparatively safe way in and out of Lowestoft was by water, as it was on a major sea route between London and northern England. By comparison, travel by road was long, slow, and in winter, cold and muddy.

Despite being in existence for 40 years and despite the fact that the surviving partners were prominent people in the town, within 50 years of its closure the Lowestoft China Factory was almost forgotten. Even the fact that most of the raw materials - clay, sand, flint, fresh running water - could still be found close at hand, was to become overlooked.

According to historian Edmund Gillingwater, Lowestoft had a total of 24 public houses by the middle of the 18th century. Even as late as the last century the Beach alone had 13 public houses.

Nothing now survives of the Lowestoft China Factory; however, several houses built by Obediah Aldred, a senior partner in the firm, can still be seen. Built opposite the factory in Bell Lane, at least one, facing the Crown Street Hall, has been identified as the home, and possibly workshop, of Mrs Stevenson and her daughter, two decorators at the factory.

LOWESTOFT, DRIFTERS c1955 L105110

LOWESTOFT, SOUTH PIER c1955 L105100

It was not until the Act of 1786 revitalizing the fishing trade that Lowestoft began to increase its population. By 1803, Lowestoft boats were earning as much as £10,000 in six weeks catching herring and mackerel alone.

John Wesley, one of the founders of the Methodist movement, first visited Lowestoft in 1764, speaking in the open air near Martin's Score. His opinion of the townspeople, 'A wilder bunch I have never met', did not deter him from returning several times afterwards.

It was not until the opening of the Norwich and Lowestoft Navigation in 1830 that Lowestoft had its first bridge. Before then, a narrow causeway between the North Sea and Lake Lothing allowed an unhindered route from the town south towards Pakefield and Kessingland.

The area around St Margaret's Plain continues to be a living piece of early Lowestoft history. Church Road, Wesley Road and Crown Street follow medieval trackways across what was once Goose Green, later called Cage Green, from St Margaret's Church towards the High Street and the nearby scores. Thurston Road was a track that went across the Green leading into Beccles Road (St Peter's Street).

Lowestoft has one of the oldest lifeboat stations in the country, if not the oldest. Founded in 1801, 20 years before the RNLI, down the years the courage of those who man these boats in the roughest of weathers has become legendary. Following names such as Swan, Capps, Spurgeon and Hook, the bravery of the Lowestoft crew continues to this day. Awards so far include 39 medals, one of the more recent recipients being John Catchpole in 1996. The present lifeboat is the 'Spirit of Lowestoft.'

King George II, it is said, was a poor sailor. In January 1737, he was caught in a violent storm while travelling to England. Laying off Lowestoft, he was rowed ashore in the royal barge. Lifted up out of the sea as he approached the beach, probably still feeling the pangs of sea-sickness, it was hardly surprising that after a short stay in the town he continued his journey to London by road!

LOWESTOFT, THE HIGHLIGHT 1890 24016

LOWESTOFT, LONDON ROAD NORTH 1891 28374

Edmund Gillingwater may have been the first Lowestoft historian; however, much of the material featured in his book published in 1790 was collected by his elder brother Isaac, whose barber shop, situated opposite the Town Chamber, was a convenient place to collect such material. Isaac also transcribed a rare book published in 1682, 'A Tryall of Witches' covering the Lowestoft Witch Trials of 1665 which is now in the Suffolk Records Office.

Many believe Lowestoft's Beach village to be older than the town on the cliff. In fact, it is less than 250 years old and developed from the expansion of the foreshore in the 1780s. Many parts of the community were built piecemeal. However, the area was prone to flooding and was effectively abandoned after the floods of 1953.

Now known as Duke's Head Street, Old Blue Anchor Lane in Lowestoft appears to have been a popular place to hold theatricals and clandestine religious meetings. Samuel Pacy held nonconformist meetings there, John Wesley is known to have preached there and David Fisher and his company of actors performed in a converted barn there in 1794.

LOWESTOFT, ROUGH SEAS, SOUTH OF CLAREMONT PIER 1922 72506

TO THE
GLORY OF GOD
AND IN MEMORY
OF THE MEN OF
THIS TOWN WHO
GAVE THEIR LIVES
IN THE GREAT WAR
'14-'19
LEST WE FORGET
THIS MONUMENT
WAS ERECTED BY
THEIR GRATEFUL
FELLOW TOWNSMEN
MISS MINNA DEACH
EVERY EVENING

The choosing by Morton Peto of waste ground south of the Navigation to build a New Town and resort at Lowestoft may have been influenced by his uncle Henry Grissell, who built the new resort of Great Yarmouth on a similar waste outside the town walls.

The Norwich and Lowestoft Navigation Bill was passed in 1827, to create a new route to the sea that would take business away from the port of Yarmouth. However, Lowestoft's new iron bridge had to come by water by way of its rival. Despite problems and devious delay tactics by an unfriendly Yarmouth the bridge was opened with great ceremony on 30 June 1830.

Lowestoft's Lake Lothing was once known as the Freshwater, said to be a popular place to fish. The locks at the Lowestoft end of the Navigation were intended to allow the Lake to remain so. Although precautions had been taken, the antics of the teredo worm, a mollusc that bored into ships' timbers, dictated otherwise and the lock became stuck in the open position contaminating the lake. It has been a sea water lake ever since.

It has become part of Lowestoft folklore that Samuel Morton Peto only paid £200 for the waste land south of the town for his New Town Estate. Recent research seems to suggest the final price was something like £500. Still a bargain, though!

Lowestoft was once smaller than Beccles. The census of 1801 gave a population of 2,332 compared with Beccles's 2,788. The Act of 1786 promoting the fishing at Lowestoft saw a steady rise in growth despite the failure of the Navigation in the 1840s. Peto's involvement with the town, however, caused the greatest increase in population, rising to 10,663 by 1861, the year he was declared bankrupt. From 1871 onwards, Lowestoft became the second largest town in Suffolk.

Although aimed at two distinct classes, the Esplanade and the Marine Parade in Lowestoft were mirror images of each other. At the head of each was its hotel followed by a row of dwellings facing east; 'superior' at the Esplanade, 'second class' at Marine Parade. The only difference was at the southern end of the new resort. The Esplanade was allowed views of the grand Wellington Terrace. Marine Parade was curtailed by the Mews.

Lowestoft has had a market since 1442. Possibly starting on the Denes (regretfully this has never been proven), it remained at the Old Market Plain until 1698, when it moved to the new Corn Cross and Town Chamber. By 1858 it had relocated to the New Market Place in Compass Street. After the construction of a new Town Hall, it was removed to the Triangle in the late 1890s and has remained in the vicinity ever since.

Morton Peto took pride in the development of his New Town in Lowestoft as well as the railway on the opposite side of Lake Lothing which brought in his wealthy clientele, yet he never gave Lowestoft a bridge befitting its new status. For 67 years, the bridge that would link both parts of the town remained the iron bridge erected in 1830.

Lowestoft's Kirkley Ham was at one time a navigable stretch of river. Late 18th-century engravings show boats moored not far away from St Peter's Church at Kirkley. With the building of the road between Horn Hill and Waveney Drive in the late 19th century, the Ham eventually became marshland.

LOWESTOFT, LONDON ROAD NORTH c1955   LI05132

LOWESTOFT, THE LIGHTHOUSE AND COTTAGES 1887 19849

The present town centre in Lowestoft is mainly the result of the selling off of the Grove Estate into plots in 1885. The estate originally stretched from today's Boots to the junction with Waveney Road. Suffolk Road, Beach Road and the aptly named Grove Road were soon laid out and by the end of the decade shops were being built. One of the first was Ebenezer Tuttle's Bon Marche store in 1888.

You could once walk across the harbour in Lowestoft and not get your feet wet. That was once the story an older generation used to tell their grandchildren. And according to photographs taken at the end of the 19th century showing the harbour crammed full of smacks, that may well have been the case. One question often cropped up. How did a boat moored near the dock manage to leave the harbour?

In many Lowestoft fishing families, first names tended to be handed down through the generations - Edmund (Mun) Capps, for example. One Edmund Capps, who died in 1945, was the last of the family to own a substantial fleet of fishing boats. Another Mun Capps lived nearby in Oxford Road - his son, Mun, emigrated to Canada and became a professional singer. He broke the mould - he had two daughters.

William Youngman may have been the first official mayor of Lowestoft, but what is forgotten is that Major Henry Steppings was the town's acting mayor, taking office from the signing of the Borough Charter by Queen Victoria in August 1885 until the official handing over two months later in November.

LOWESTOFT, A CONVALESCENT HOME 1887 19856

1903 was a spectacular year for Lowestoft. The year included the opening of the Claremont Pier, the Yarmouth rail line, the opening of the Royal Norfolk and Suffolk Yacht Club by Sir Claud Hamilton, and the opening of the municipal tramway.

The weirdest vehicle ever made by Brooke's of Lowestoft was the famous Swan car, built in 1910 for a wealthy eccentric Scottish engineer who lived in India. Complete with a carved head and body of a swan, it had a horn made of eight organ pipes. It disappeared for decades before suddenly turning up at an auction in this country. It has since been restored.

During the naval bombardment of Lowestoft in April 1916, a 12-inch shell went through a terrace of 13 houses in Kent Road, ending up in the bedroom of the last house without exploding. The terrace still survives today.

There were plans to reopen Lowestoft's St Luke's Hospital (the old Empire Hotel) in the early 1950s. Requisitioned during the Second World War, plans had been made to reopen it as a hospital after the war. However, it was decided to demolish the building in 1958. The site became St Mary's RC Primary School.

LOWESTOFT, THE HARBOUR FROM THE SOUTH PIER c1955   LI05131

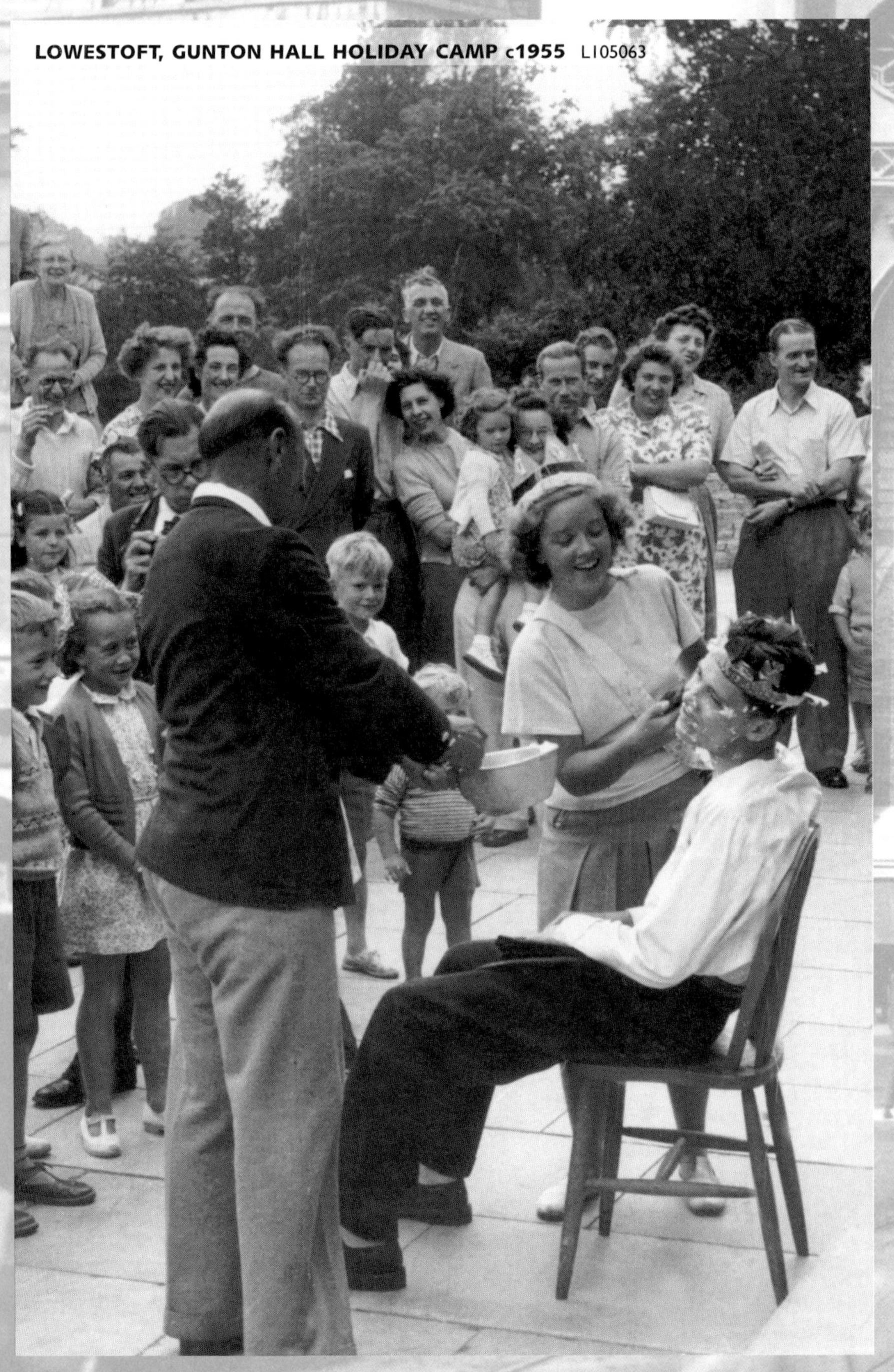

LOWESTOFT, GUNTON HALL HOLIDAY CAMP c1955   L105063

Lowestoft's second sea wall was also used for motor sport. The building started in 1923 and was completed in 1925. From 1927 a bus service ran from south Lowestoft to the wall finishing in the weeks leading up to the outbreak of war. Neglected during the war, the sea wall eventually collapsed in 1946.

ARP wardens were proposed for Lowestoft as early as 1937. With unrest in Europe, the government of the day was urging towns like Lowestoft to organise air-raid precautions including wardens and shelters. During this time the town was also benefiting from the increase in orders for shipping and engineering.

LOWESTOFT, BELLE VUE PARK 1890 24014a

Most of Lowestoft's old buildings were lost in the clearances of the 1950s and 1960s, the most ancient being Old Market Place, Mariner's Street, Duke's Head Street and White Horse Street. Chapel Street and Gun Lane were also lost, as were properties relating to the China Factory. A popular quip of the time was that the Borough had done more damage to the town than the Germans!

The Britten Centre in Lowestoft is aptly named after one of Britain's most famous composers. Feet away from today's hustle and bustle in its town centre entrance, in September 1923 a nine-year-old Benjamin Britten was brought, complete with his new prep school uniform and under protest, to have his portrait taken in the studio of Christopher Wilson. The site of the studio, 91 London Road North, is now part of Dorothy Perkins. Benjamin's father, Robert, was a dentist in Lowestoft.

LOWESTOFT, THE VIEW FROM PAKEFIELD 1890 24022

LOWESTOFT, LONDON ROAD NORTH 1896 37924

LOWESTOFT, CORTON, THE CLYFFE 1893   32260

LOWESTOFT, LONDON ROAD SOUTH 1896   37925

LOWESTOFT QUIZ QUESTIONS

1. In the late 19th century there were once two crescents in north
    Lowestoft, both now gone.
    Where were they?

2. Two public houses in Lowestoft were demolished on the
    Triangle in the 1880s to make way for a proposed town hall.
    What eventually replaced them?

3. In 1643, following the quelling of unrest in Lowestoft, Oliver
    Cromwell stayed at the Swan Inn.
    Where was it?

4. Today's High Light in Lowestoft is at the highest point of the
    High Street. In 1608, an even earlier 'highlight' was recorded
    elsewhere in the town - where?

5. Ada Roe was the longest surviving Lowestoft resident.
    How old was she when she died in 1970?

6. The Public Library in Lowestoft was destroyed by bombing in March 1941. In 1951 it was moved to Suffolk Road from which house in the High Street?

7. The London Road Baptist Church in Lowestoft, although demolished in the 1970s, still exists.
    Where is it now?

8. Until recent times, Lowestoft was on two major trading routes. Which were they?

9. Which Lowestoft pier was never built?

10. Lowestoft China is famous the world over; where was the China Factory, and what is it now?

11. Robert Browne, a partner in the Lowestoft China Factory, is supposed to have secreted himself in the Bow factory in London to learn some of its processes.
    In what was he supposed to have been hidden?

LOWESTOFT, OULTON BROAD 1919 69308

12. During the widening of the High Street at the start of the last century, what was discovered opposite what is now the oldest house in Lowestoft?

13. In Lowestoft, Brooke's are remembered as builders of yachts, trawlers and naval vessels, as well as for early car production. What other examples of their work can be seen in Station Square and the High Street?

14. The Claremont Pier, the Royal Norfolk & Suffolk Yacht Club, the Lowestoft to Yarmouth railway and Lowestoft's municipal tram service were all opened in the one year.
Which year?

15. Looking back to the First World War, 149-151 London Road South, Lowestoft, and Windsor Gallery on the corner of Freemantle Road and London Road South both have one thing in common. What is it?

LOWESTOFT, WARREN COTTAGES 1891 28380

16. Next to 176 High Street, Lowestoft, there is a
    paved area with trees. What was once on the site?

17. The Waller Raid on Lowestoft occurred in January 1942.
    Of the 70 killed and 114 injured, who received the greater
    casualties - civilian or service personnel?

18. Although it received borough status in 1885, Lowestoft
    was a municipal corporation for less than 100 years.
    Why?

19. Morling's rebuilt their music shop at 149-151 London
    Road North, Lowestoft, after the Second World War.
    It was officially reopened by a famous classical pianist.
    Who?

20. As Infirmary Plain, St Margaret's Plain housed the
    town's first purpose-built infirmary in Lowestoft.
    What was it known as before then?

LOWESTOFT, THE HARBOUR c1955 L105072

21. Two Lowestoft churches were lost in London
    Road North - firstly in 1956 and then in 1974.
    Which ones?

22. The Belle Vue Park in north Lowestoft once had
    a pagoda bandstand.
    What replaced it after the war?

23. The future author of 'Heart of Darkness' and 'Lord Jim' landed
    at Lowestoft in 1878 as a young seaman unable to speak
    English. Staying at the Crown and Anchor in the High Street,
    his introduction to the English language was the old Lowestoft
    dialect.
    Who was he?

24. Victorian photographers took several scenes in London Road
    North, Lowestoft, in the 1890s which show the shopping
    parade on the site between today's Gordon Road and the
    Marina. On the opposite site, on the left of the picture, is
    usually a small, almost inconspicuous castellated single-storey
    building.
    What was it?

25. The same natural disaster occurred twice in the last 125 years at Lowestoft; firstly in Queen Victoria's Golden Jubilee year and secondly in the Coronation year of our present Queen. What type of natural disaster was it?

26. Why is 1802 a particularly interesting year to devotees of Lowestoft China?

LOWESTOFT, THE HOSPITAL 1893 32255

LOWESTOFT, FROM THE DENES 1896 37942

27. Lowestoft's first market place dates from 1442 and lasted until 1698. From around 1857 to the 1890s the market was held at New Market Plain (also known as the New Market Place). Where was this?

28. Today, there is a Bon Marche store in Lowestoft town centre opposite Tesco's supermarket which was opened in the last two years. Where was the first Bon Marche in the town and when did it open?

29. Although the Lowestoft China Factory is long gone, the house of at least one of its decorators still survives and can be found opposite a public hall which was once a theatre. Where?

LOWESTOFT, SPARROW'S NEST 1922 72509

LOWESTOFT, SPARROW'S NEST, THE BOWLING GREEN 1922 72510

30. The name 'score' found around Lowestoft refers to paths or tracks literally 'scored' or cut into the cliff face. Lowestoft's southern-most score just managed to survive the Second World War but eventually disappeared to be come part of the modern police station and magistrate's court.
    What was its name?

31. Lowestoft's first coat of arms can be found on three buildings: one in Crown Street, one over the entrance to Jarrold's stationery shop in Beach Road.
    Where is the third one?

32. The Lowestoft author George Borrow lived at Oulton. In 1885, after his death, some of the estate, notably along Hall Road, was sold off and eventually built on.
    What is the area called today?

33. Lowestoft once had a Corn Cross. Where?

34. In 1935, the year of King George V's Silver Jubilee, Lowestoft also celebrated its golden jubilee as a borough. Both were held in one week-long celebration in July of that year. Despite a fabulous turnout, the town got itself into trouble. Why?

35. Lowestoft's South Battery was in front of Maid's Acre.
What is on the site now?

36. Although Lowestoft's fishing boat numbers went into four
digits, they never went beyond LT 1299.
Why?

37. David Fisher brought his company of actors to Lowestoft in
1794. In the first half of the 19th century the Fisher family
erected two buildings, both of which survive.
Where and what are they?

38. The Universal Directory for 1794 and other early publications
often speak of the 'hanging gardens of Lowestoft'.
What were they?

39. With the arrival of the railway, Oulton Broad became
the haunt of yachtsmen and gentleman fishermen and
expanded accordingly.
In what year did it become part of the borough of Lowestoft?

LOWESTOFT, THE ROYAL HOTEL 1922 72497

LOWESTOFT, THE SWING BRIDGE c1955 LI05085

40. The biggest fire in Lowestoft's history occurred in 1645.
    Where did it start?

41. Lowestoft has a long tradition of naval seamen. In 1665 two
    of them, Sir Thomas Allin and Rear Admiral Riches Utber,
    both fought the Dutch in the same engagement on the
    German Ocean.
    What battle was it and what is the German Ocean known
    as today?

42. Edmund Gillingwater wrote the first history of Lowestoft in 1790. But who collected the material he used?

43. One of the largest public displays of Lowestoft China could be seen at one time at Norwich Castle museum. Where, at the time of writing, can the largest public display be seen today?

LOWESTOFT, GUNTON CHURCH 1896 37940

44. On the cliff top in Belle Vue Park, Lowestoft, are cannon that
    face out to sea. Why?

LOWESTOFT, PUNCH AND JUDY, CHILDREN'S CORNER c1955 L105079

LOWESTOFT, KENSINGTON GARDENS 1922 72508

LOWESTOFT, KENSINGTON GARDENS 1922 72508

45. King George II landed at Lowestoft after a rough sea journey
   from Holland. He stayed at the house of John Jex opposite
   the Town Chamber. Also known as Chaston House, what is it
   today?

46. Brewer William Youngman was the first mayor of Lowestoft.
   Who was the second mayor?

LOWESTOFT, MARINE PARADE 1919 69307

47. Pakefield is an ancient place, much of which has fallen into the sea. Which is now the oldest public house in Pakefield and where is it?

48. Since December 2004, Lowestoft has had a new landmark. What is it?

49. Two important buildings in Lowestoft were designed by John Thomas for Sir Samuel Morton Peto. One was Somerleyton Hall, what was the other one?

50. Where was Old Blue Anchor Lane in Lowestoft?

LOWESTOFT, THE YACHT BASIN AND THE HARBOUR 1921 71699

LOWESTOFT, HIGH LIGHTHOUSE 1921 71705

LOWESTOFT QUIZ ANSWERS

1. a) The Crescent, located between Yarmouth Road and Park Road, and b) the Marina in London Road North, which lost its northern entrance in the 1980s with the eastern extension of Gordon Road and the building of Lowestoft's first multi-storey car park.

2. The Triangle Market.

3. On the corner of the High Street and Mariner's Score, now 41 and 42 High Street.

4. The northern side of Mariner's Score.

5. She died at the age of 111, just short of her 112th birthday.

6. 27 High Street, also known as East Holme or the North Flint House. It was once the home of Sir Thomas Allin.

7. Still known as the London Road Baptist Church, it moved to a new building on the corner of the Avenue and London Road South.

8. The North Sea, the trading route between Newcastle upon Tyne and London; and from 1847, the railway, which opened up inland markets to the Lowestoft fishing fleet.

9. The proposed North Pier near Lighthouse Score. The first sod was turned by the Duke of Cambridge in December 1899, but the project never got further than that.

10. The site of the China Factory is now partly under the Crown Artist Brush factory car park in Crown Street West.

11. A barrel.

12. Medieval undercrofts or cellars.

13. Shop fronts. The most complete being 56-57 High Street. Remains of two others can also be traced at 11 Station Square (the old Ford Jenkins studio) and Panda Book Shop in the High Street.

14. 1903.

15. They were both damaged in the naval bombardment of Lowestoft on the morning of 25 April 1916.

16. The Jubilee Stores. The public house received a direct hit in a raid in May 1943. Many of those who died in the building were never found.

17. It was estimated that of the killed and injured most were civilian, and mainly at Waller's Restaurant.

18. In 1974, with the rearranging of county and local authority boundaries, Lowestoft became the administrative centre for Waveney District Council, an area that included Beccles, Bungay, Southwold and Halesworth.

19. Benno Moisewitch.

20. Cage Green.

21. The Central Methodist Church on the corner of the Marina, damaged during the Second World War and demolished in 1956; and the London Road Baptist Church, which went in 1973 to make way for the present Boots store.

22. The Royal Naval Patrol Service memorial which was unveiled in 1953.

23. Joseph Conrad, or to give him his Polish name - Josef Teodor Korzeniowski.

24. A prefabricated photographic studio. Erected in 1863 by local pioneering photographer Michael Barrett, it continued in use until around 1896. A shoe shop is now on the site.

LOWESTOFT QUIZ ANSWERS

25. Floods. Firstly in November 1897 and secondly in January/February 1953.

26. 1802 was the year the surviving partners in the Factory disposed of their remaining assets, including the Factory itself. Phillip Walker sold off his fishing interests in this year, and 1802 appears to be the last date found on ceramics decorated by Robert Allen, who may have also given up his shop at that date.

27. Compass Street. Now the Town Hall car park.

28. The first 'Bon Marche' in Lowestoft was the department store opened in 1888 by Ebenezer Tuttle on the corner of Suffolk Road and London Road North. The store finally closed in 1981.

29. Opposite Crown Street Hall, Crown Street West.

30. Frosts Alley Score.

31. On the Turret Buildings on the corner of Waveney Road and London Road North.

32. The Rock Estate.

33. On the site of today's Town Hall, roughly where its entrance is today.

34. The King's jubilee was, in fact, celebrated nationally in June 1935, not July.

35. The site of the Battery is now covered by the Somerfield multi-storey car park and the roundabout at the foot of Old Nelson Street.

36. The number 13 is considered unlucky, therefore there was no registration LT 1300 onwards. As numbers became vacant, they were reused as needed.

37. Crown Street Hall, built 1812 as a Fisher theatre and Marine Terrace, opposite Westgates in London Road North, and built in the 1840s.

38. The phrase refers to the gardens of the houses on the cliff side of the High Street as seen from the sea. Laid out in terraces, an assortment of flowers, bushes, trees and summer houses made for a spectacular sight when viewed from afar.

39. 1919.

40. The Great Fire of 1645 started at a fish house at the foot of 1, High Street, close to Arnold's Walk.

41. The conflict was the Battle of Lowestoft which took place on 3 June 1665. The German Ocean is now known as the North Sea.

42. His elder brother Isaac, who was a barber in the High Street.

43. The Lowestoft Museum at Broad House, Nicholas Everitt Park.

44. The cannon commemorate the North Battery which was established during the Dutch Wars of the 17th century and strengthened in 1782.

45. Tinkerbelle's bridalwear shop, 45 High Street.

46. The architect John Louth Clemence, who remained in the town after Peto left Lowestoft following his bankruptcy.

47. The Trowel and Hammer in Pakefield Street.

48. Gulliver - the largest wind turbine in the country. At 126 metres high, it is taller than Norwich Cathedral. Each of its blades are 92 metres in length.

49. Wellington Terrace.

50. Dukes Head Street.

GOUDHURST, MEASURING THE HOPS 1904 52571

GENERAL HISTORY QUIZ QUESTIONS

1. Which 20th-century Prime Minister was a proficient bricklayer and a member of the union?

2. In Victorian times, what powerful substance did many fashionable society ladies use to spice up their afternoon tea parties?

3. What was the first battle of the English Civil War on 23 October 1642?

4. Who was Queen Victoria's first Prime Minister?

5.   Which Michigan-born dentist was arrested in Canada for the murder of his wife in London?

6.   For what crime was Titus Oates pilloried in the stocks and flogged every year?

7.   What crime was committed by Burke and Hare?

8.   What language was Elizabeth I not fluent in? German, French, Latin, or Italian?

9.   In 1834 six Dorset farm labourers were transported to Australia. By what name are these men usually known?

HORNING, ON THE BROADS 1902 48108

MARKET DRAYTON, MARKET DAY 1911 63338

10. At which battle was Richard III slain?

11. Who was the first Prime Minister to live at Chequers?

12. Who was the leader of the Women's Social and Political Union?

13. What year were women granted the vote on the Isle of Man?
    1881, 1902, 1912, or 1946?

RHYL, DONKEYS ON THE SANDS 1891 29151

14. Which king signed the Magna Carta in 1215 at Runnymede?

15. In which city was the infamous Peterloo Massacre on 16 August 1819?

16. Who were the mother and father of Elizabeth I?

17. Before the French Revolution in 1789, who is reported to have said 'Let them eat cake'?

18. Who wore two shirts in which to be executed, and why?

NEWQUAY, THE HARBOUR 1894 33522

19. Which queen was known as Bloody Mary?

20. Who was the only English pope?

21. Which British king married May of Teck?

22. At the outbreak of World War I, who was the British Prime Minister?

23. What great structure, designed by Joseph Paxton, was built in 1851?

24. What were the names of the two princes believed to have been murdered in the Tower of London in 1483?

25. What unusual accident eventually caused the death of the Prince of Wales, eldest son of George II?

26. Which of Dickens's novels depicts the struggles and strife of factory workers in Victorian England?

EVERSLEY, THE WHITE HART 1906 57011

CASTLETON, SPEEDWELL CAVERN 1909 61785

27. How old was William Shakespeare when he got married? 24, 25, 19, or 18?

28. What crime occurred on 8 August 1963 that shocked public opinion in Britain?

29. Who had to hide in an oak tree to save his life after a military defeat?

30. After Henry VIII's Dissolution of the Monasteries, what are some of the new owners of the monastery buildings rumoured to have done with some of the illuminated manuscripts they found?

KING'S LYNN, HIGH STREET 1908 60023

BOURNEMOUTH, INVALID'S WALK 1900 45226

31. In July 1888, 1,500 female employees went on strike at a factory at Bow in East London. What did they manufacture?

32. Who was the Irish saint who legend says saw the Loch Ness Monster in Scotland?
St Columba, St Patrick, St Andrew, or St Aidan?

33. Which English woman made this prophecy:
'Carriages without horses shall go, And accidents fill the world with woe. Around the world thoughts shall fly, In the twinkling of an eye.'?

34. Which tax was levied between 1696 and 1851?

35. How long did the Hundred Years' War last? 116 years, 94 years, 100 years, or 108 years?

36. Who was called the 'Old Pretender'?

37. In 1629 William Harvey published the details of a discovery he had made. What was it?

38. Put these wars and battles in the order in which they took place:
    A. The Battle of Agincourt
    B. The Battle of Hastings
    C. Marston Moor
    D. Wars of the Roses

39. In British army slang, what was a 'dead man'?

40. When was the Poll Tax first introduced in England?

SAFFRON WALDEN, FRY'S GARDEN 1907 58821

CLOVELLY, POST OFFICE, TRANSFER OF MAIL 1936 87551

41. Who was the first Prime Minister of Britain?

42. What is pannage?

43. What were the Welshmen of the Rebecca Riots, who dressed up as women, protesting against?

44. How many people did the 1715 Riot Act have to be read to, in order for them to be guilty of a felony, and liable to the punishment of death? 6, 12, 27, or 250?

CHALFORD, THE VILLAGE 1910 62713

45. What was the joint stock company, the South Sea Company, set up in 1711 to trade in?

46. In the Middle Ages, a split stick was used by royal officials to record sums of money paid. Notches were cut on it representing payments. What was it called?

EASTBOURNE, THE PIER 1925 77946

47. When did the Union Jack achieve its present pattern?

48. In 1752, September 2 was followed by September 14. What was the name of the new calendar system that involved this adjustment?

NEWBY BRIDGE, THE SWAN HOTEL 1914 67414

49. Coffee houses were patronised by literary giants such as
    Dryden, Johnson, and Pope. How many coffee houses were
    there in London in the 18th century?
    10, 50, 250, or 1800?

50. Who was the first British Prime Minister to live at 10 Downing
    Street?

TENBY 1890 28091

GENERAL HISTORY QUIZ ANSWERS

1. Winston Churchill.

2. Opium.

3. Edgehill.

4. Lord Melbourne.

5. Dr Crippen. He buried her body in the basement of his London house.

6. For giving false evidence against Catholics.

7. They murdered people and sold their corpses to unscrupulous surgeons for dissection.

8. German.

9. The Tolpuddle Martyrs.

10. The Battle of Bosworth Field.

11. Lloyd George.

12. Emmeline Pankhurst.

13. 1881.

14. King John.

15. Manchester.

16. Henry VIII and Anne Boleyn.

17. Marie Antoinette.

18. Charles I. The weather was cold and he did not want to be seen shivering.

19. Mary I, the daughter of Henry VIII and Catherine of Aragon. She married Philip II of Spain, and was a devout Catholic. She earned her nickname from her persecution of Protestants.

20. Adrian IV, born Nicholas Brakespeare in 1100.

21. George V (she was known in this country as Mary).

22. Herbert Asquith.

23. The Crystal Palace.

24. Edward V and his brother Richard Duke of York, the sons of Edward IV.

25. He was hit on the head by a cricket ball.

GENERAL HISTORY QUIZ ANSWERS

26. 'Hard Times', published in 1854.

27. 18.

28. The Great Train Robbery.

29. Charles II.

30. They used them as lavatory paper.

31. Matches. They worked at the Bryant and May factory.

32. St Columba, born cAD521.

33. Mother Shipton, born in Norfolk in 1485.

34. Window Tax, which was payable on a house with more than six windows.

35. 116 years, between 1337 and 1453.

36. James III (the son of James II). In 1715 he gathered together a force of 10,000 men and invaded England. The Jacobites fought their way as far as Preston, where they were dispersed.

37. The circulation of the blood. He was physician extraordinary to James I.

38. B (1066) A (1415) D (1455-85) C (1644).

39. An empty bottle.

40. In 1222, on every person over the age of 14.

41. Robert Walpole. As first Lord of the Treasury between 1721 and 1742 he presided over the cabinet.

42. The right of tenants to graze their swine in the woods of a manor.

43. They destroyed turnpike houses, being unhappy about the levels of tolls.

44. 12.

45. Slaves in Latin America.

46. A tally.

47. In 1801, when the cross of St Patrick was added to the crosses of St George and St Andrew.

48. The Gregorian Calendar.

49. 1800.

50. Sir Robert Walpole (1676-1745).

Ottakar's Bookshops

Ottakar's bookshops, the first of which opened in Brighton in 1988, can now be found in over 130 towns and cities across the United Kingdom. Expansion was gradual throughout the 1990s, but the chain has expanded rapidly in recent years, with many new shop openings and the acquisition of shops from James Thin and Hammicks.

Ottakar's has always known that a shop's local profile is as important, if not more important, than the chain's national profile, and has encouraged its staff to make their shops a part of the local community, tailoring stock to suit the area and forging links with local schools and businesses.

Local history has always been a strong area for Ottakar's, and the company has published its own award winning local history titles, based on text written by its customers, in recent years.

With a reputation for friendly, intelligent and enthusiastic booksellers, warm, inviting shops with an excellent range of books and related products, Ottakar's is now one of the UK's most popular booksellers. In 2003 and then again in 2004 it won the prestigious Best Bookselling Company of the Year Award at the British Book Awards.

Ottakar's has commissioned The Francis Frith Collection to create a series of town history books similar to this volume, as well as a range of stylish gift products, all illustrated with historical photographs.

Participating Ottakar's bookshops can be found in the following towns and cities:

Aberdeen	Fareham	Ormskirk
Abergavenny	Farnham	Petersfield
Aberystwyth	Folkestone	Portsmouth
Andover	Glasgow	Poole
Ashford	Gloucester	Redhill
Ayr	Greenwich	St Albans
Banbury	Grimsby	St Andrews
Barnstaple	Guildford	St Neots
Basildon	Harrogate	St Helier
Berkhamsted	Hastings	Salisbury
Bishop's Stortford	Haywards Heath	Sheffield
Boston	Hemel Hempstead	Stafford
Brentwood	High Wycombe	Staines
Bromley	Horsham	Stevenage
Bury St Edmunds	Huddersfield	Sutton Coldfield
Camberley	Inverness	Teddington
Canterbury	Isle of Wight	Tenterden
Carmarthen	Kendal	Tiverton
Chatham	King's Lynn	Torquay
Chelmsford	Kirkcaldy	Trowbridge
Cheltenham	Lancaster	Truro
Cirencester	Lincoln	Tunbridge Wells
Coventry	Llandudno	Twickenham
Crawley	Loughborough	Walsall
Darlington	Lowestoft	Wilmslow and
Dorchester	Luton	Alderley Edge
Douglas, Isle of Man	Lymington	Wells
Dumfries	Maidenhead	Weston-super-Mare
Dundee	Maidstone	Windsor
East Grinstead	Market Harborough	Witney
Eastbourne	Milton Keynes	Woking
Elgin	Newport	Worcester
Enfield	Newton Abbot	Yeovil
Epsom	Norwich	
Falkirk	Oban	

Francis Frith
Pioneer Victorian Photographer

Francis Frith, founder of the world-famous photographic archive, was a complex and multi-talented man. A devout Quaker and a highly successful Victorian businessman, he was philosophical by nature and pioneering in outlook. By 1855 he had already established a wholesale grocery business in Liverpool, and sold it for the astonishing sum of £200,000, which is the equivalent today of over £15,000,000. Now in his thirties, and captivated by the new science of photography, Frith set out on a series of pioneering journeys up the Nile and to the Near East.

INTRIGUE AND EXPLORATION

He was the first photographer to venture beyond the sixth cataract of the Nile. Africa was still the mysterious 'Dark Continent', and Stanley and Livingstone's historic meeting was a decade into the future. The conditions for picture taking confound belief. He laboured for hours in his wicker dark-room in the sweltering heat of the desert, while the volatile chemicals fizzed dangerously in their trays. Back in London he exhibited his photographs and was 'rapturously cheered' by members of the Royal Society. His reputation as a photographer was made overnight.

VENTURE OF A LIFE-TIME

By the 1870s the railways had threaded their way across the country, and Bank Holidays and half-day Saturdays had been made obligatory by Act of Parliament. All of a sudden the working man and his family were able to enjoy days out, take holidays, and see a little more of the world.

With typical business acumen, Francis Frith foresaw that these new tourists would enjoy having souvenirs to commemorate their days out. For the next thirty years he travelled the country by train and by pony and trap, producing fine photographs of seaside resorts and beauty spots that were keenly bought by millions of Victorians. These prints were painstakingly pasted into family albums and pored over during the dark nights of winter, rekindling precious memories of summer excursions. Frith's studio was soon supplying retail shops all over the country, and by 1890 F Frith & Co had become the greatest specialist photographic publishing company in the world, with over 2,000 sales outlets, and pioneered the picture postcard.

FRANCIS FRITH'S LEGACY

Francis Frith had died in 1898 at his villa in Cannes, his great project still growing. By 1970 the archive he created contained over a third of a million pictures showing 7,000 British towns and villages.

Frith's legacy to us today is of immense significance and value, for the magnificent archive of evocative photographs he created provides a unique record of change in the cities, towns and villages throughout Britain over a century and more. Frith and his fellow studio photographers revisited locations many times down the years to update their views, compiling for us an enthralling and colourful pageant of British life and character.

We are fortunate that Frith was dedicated to recording the minutiae of everyday life. For it is this sheer wealth of visual data, the painstaking chronicle of changes in dress, transport, street layouts, buildings, housing and landscape that captivates us so much today, offering us a powerful link with the past and with the lives of our ancestors.

Computers have now made it possible for Frith's many thousands of images to be accessed almost instantly. The archive offers every one of us an opportunity to examine the places where we and our families have lived and worked down the years. Its images, depicting our shared past, are now bringing pleasure and enlightenment to millions around the world a century and more after his death.

For further information visit: www.francisfrith.co.uk